DEFINING EVENTS
of the Twenty-First Century

# POP CULTURE AND ENTERTAINMENT

## in the Twenty-First Century

by Tammy Gagne

ReferencePoint
Press®

San Diego, CA

© 2020 ReferencePoint Press, Inc.
Printed in the United States

For more information, contact:
ReferencePoint Press, Inc.
PO Box 27779
San Diego, CA 92198
www.ReferencePointPress.com

LIBRARY OF CONGRESS CATALOGING-IN-PUBLICATION DATA

Names: Gagne, Tammy, author.
Title: Pop culture and entertainment in the twenty-first century / by Tammy
    Gagne.
Description: San Diego, CA : ReferencePoint Press, Inc., [2020] | Series:
    Defining events of the twenty-first century | Audience: Grades 9-12. |
    Includes bibliographical references and index.
Identifiers: LCCN 2019000778 (print) | LCCN 2019012896 (ebook) | ISBN
    9781682826041 (ebook) | ISBN 9781682826027 (hardcover)
Subjects: LCSH: Popular culture--United States--History--21st
    century--Juvenile literature. | Entertainment events--United
    States--History--21st century--Juvenile literature. | United
    States--Civilization--21st century--Juvenile literature.
Classification: LCC E169.12 (ebook) | LCC E169.12 .G34 2020 (print) | DDC
    306.0973/0905--dc23
LC record available at https://lccn.loc.gov/2019000778

# CONTENTS

IMPORTANT EVENTS                                        4

INTRODUCTION                                            6
Celebrating Pop Culture

CHAPTER 1                                              10
Events That Changed the World of Music

CHAPTER 2                                              26
Television and Movies
in the Twenty-First Century

CHAPTER 3                                              42
Popular Books of the Twenty-First Century

CHAPTER 4                                              56
Sporting Events That Have Defined
the Twenty-First Century

Source Notes                                           70
For Further Research                                   74
Index                                                  76
Image Credits                                          79
About the Author                                       80

# IMPORTANT EVENTS

**2000**
The reality show *Survivor* premieres on CBS.

**2005**
YouTube is launched, revolutionizing the way people share and watch videos online.

**2002**
Halle Berry becomes the first African American to win an Oscar for Best Actress for her work in the film *Monster's Ball*.

**2007**
The sitcom *The Big Bang Theory* premieres on CBS.

**2004**
Pixar releases the first *Incredibles* movie.

**2008**
Michael Phelps earns eight gold medals in the Summer Olympics, setting a new record for the most gold medals won during a single Olympics.

2000  2002  2004  2006  2008

**2003**
LeBron James joins the Cleveland Cavaliers basketball team straight out of high school.

**2006**
*Hannah Montana* premieres on the Disney Channel, launching the music career of its star, Miley Cyrus.

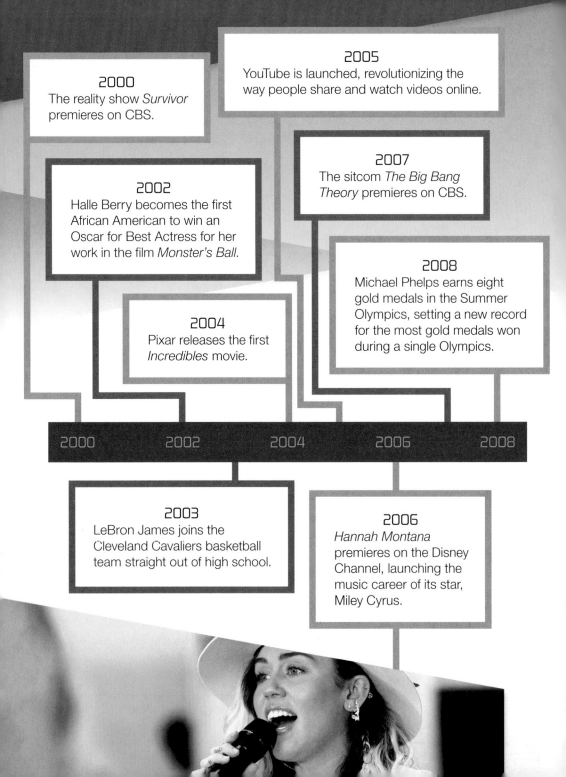

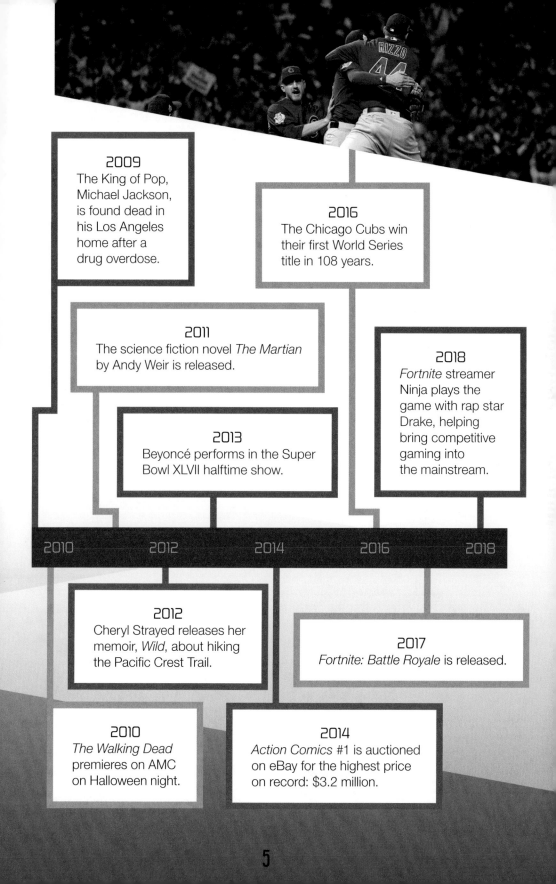

**2009**
The King of Pop, Michael Jackson, is found dead in his Los Angeles home after a drug overdose.

**2016**
The Chicago Cubs win their first World Series title in 108 years.

**2011**
The science fiction novel *The Martian* by Andy Weir is released.

**2018**
*Fortnite* streamer Ninja plays the game with rap star Drake, helping bring competitive gaming into the mainstream.

**2013**
Beyoncé performs in the Super Bowl XLVII halftime show.

2010    2012    2014    2016    2018

**2012**
Cheryl Strayed releases her memoir, *Wild*, about hiking the Pacific Crest Trail.

**2017**
*Fortnite: Battle Royale* is released.

**2010**
*The Walking Dead* premieres on AMC on Halloween night.

**2014**
*Action Comics* #1 is auctioned on eBay for the highest price on record: $3.2 million.

# Celebrating Pop Culture

W hen Comic-Con began in San Diego, California, in the 1970s, the convention drew a fairly small crowd. It brought together about 300 people eager to celebrate their favorite comic books and characters. Over time, though, the event grew dramatically in both size and scope. By the twenty-first century, Comic-Con was filling a massive convention center. It drew more than 130,000 attendants in 2017. These dedicated fans typically show up in elaborate costumes, attend celebrity panels, and spend money on merchandise and souvenirs. To some, it might seem like a lot of fuss about things that are rather insignificant. Sure, comic books are popular collector's items, and clearly the superhero trend at the movies has been big in recent years—but do these things really justify such a huge gathering?

It might help the skeptics to understand that Comic-Con, and the many smaller conventions now held around the world, are about much more than comic books.

> **"If it matters in pop culture today, it is happening at Comic-Con."[1]**
>
> —Consultant Jeremy Pepper, 2018

Huge crowds of pop culture fans attend Comic-Con each year. They wait in long lines to get the first look at upcoming movies, television shows, and comics.

Of course comics and graphic novels are still a huge part of the lure of the conventions, but these events also cater to fans of popular movies, television shows, and video games that have nothing to do with superheroes. As consultant Jeremy Pepper wrote in 2018, "If it matters in pop culture today, it is happening at Comic-Con."[1]

## The Importance of Entertainment

Experts have noticed that Comic-Con and other events do more than simply celebrate the entertainment that dominates popular culture. These events have also come to influence what becomes most popular. Henry Jenkins is the USC Provost Professor of Communication, Journalism, Cinematic Arts, and Education. When interviewed by Pepper, Jenkins pointed out that the increasing diversity the public is seeing in pop culture is a result of Comic-Con's growing audience—and of the entertainment industry's decision to pay attention to diversity in its fans. "The success of *Wonder Woman* and *Black Panther* were almost certainly born here," he asserted.[2]

Predicting which movies, books, and music will become most popular has always led to extensive discussion and study. Entertainment is a significant part of the modern world economy, raking in an enormous amount of money through the sales of movie tickets, books, downloads, and merchandise. Sporting events, too, play a substantial role in pop culture, with their fans producing the massive amount of revenue that helps pay the salaries of top athletes In recent years, gaming has become a larger and larger part of the world of pop culture. Competitive gaming, known as E-Sports, has broken into the mainstream, and the top players and streamers have become celebrities themselves.

Many of the unique features of pop culture and entertainment in the twenty-first century have come about thanks to the internet. By the turn of the century, the number of people with high-speed home internet was beginning to rise, and within a few years the vast majority of people in developed nations had it. The result has been an explosion of creativity, sharing, and collaboration. Video streaming websites, most notably YouTube, have made it possible for an individual to make their own show using little more than a basic computer and a cheap camera. Media creators of all kinds have embraced the capabilities created by the internet, changing not just the content they create but also how it can be accessed.

# Pop Culture and People's Lives

While some moments garner the spotlight for a short time, others have a more lasting effect on consumers and fans. Many people will long remember 2016, for example, as the year that took so many musical icons—from David Bowie to Leonard Cohen. Prince Rogers Nelson, known to his millions of fans simply as Prince, died on April 21, 2016, at the age of 57. Perhaps one of the reasons that his death was felt so universally was that he held a deep understanding of how profoundly his craft affected people. "Music is spirit, it's therapy," he once said. "It makes me feel a certain way, and if played with conviction and soul, the same thing occurs in other people."[3]

> "Music is spirit, it's therapy. It makes me feel a certain way, and if played with conviction and soul, the same thing occurs in other people."[3]
>
> —Prince, 2004

Books, movies, television, sports, and gaming also have a way of lessening people's stress and bringing joy into their everyday lives. These forms of entertainment offer lighthearted fun, but they also provide important opportunities. During her time in the White House, former First Lady Michelle Obama would often make appearances on popular television shows. She even danced on *The Tonight Show* with Jimmy Fallon and sang with James Corden on his show *Carpool Karaoke*. While some people saw her as an especially good sport, others wondered why she embraced pop culture so willingly. During a 2016 interview with *Variety*, she explained, "For so many people, television and movies may be the only way they understand people who aren't like them."[4]

# Chapter 1

# Events That Changed the World of Music

Music has been a driving force of pop culture for as long as artists have been recording songs. Popular artists have influenced dance, fashion, film, and even the perfume industry. At the dawn of the twenty-first century, hip-hop, pop, and rock were the dominating musical genres. One could rarely turn on a radio without hearing a song from Britney Spears's blockbuster 2000 album, *Oops! . . . I Did It Again*. The album sold 1.3 million copies in its first week. It held the record for the most sales in one week for an album by a female artist until Adele released *25* more than fifteen years later. At only eighteen years old, Spears became an instant hit with young girls. They wanted to sing like her, dress like her, and attend her concerts.

The dream of becoming a pop star certainly wasn't a new one. Each generation has spent its fair share of time in front of mirrors with hairbrushes or other pretend microphones in hand, belting out favorite songs. In 2002, a new television show called *American Idol* aimed to make a handful of those dreams come true. The premise was simple yet thrilling. Judges for the show would travel across the country, holding large-scale auditions for amateur singers. Aspiring stars showed up in droves, some demonstrating jaw-dropping talent

*American Idol* became a major part of music culture in the United States in the early twenty-first century. It was one of the nation's top TV shows for more than a decade.

and others revealing a clear and often ear-splitting overconfidence in their musical ability. Each singer chosen to become a contestant on the show received a golden ticket, which meant a trip to Hollywood to compete at the next level. Eventually, the television viewers would take over in judging the performers, phoning in votes for their favorites. Dramatic eliminations would take place each week until only one performer was left—the American Idol.

When the show's first season came down to just two contestants, Kelly Clarkson and Justin Guarini, 23 million viewers tuned in to watch the live results. With 58 percent of the vote, Clarkson nabbed the title, along with the accompanying record contract given to the show's winner. Just seconds after host Ryan Seacrest announced her name, Clarkson had to perform her first single. "A Moment Like This" shot to the top of the Billboard Hot 100 and held that spot on the chart for two weeks.

In a 2013 interview with *CBS This Morning* cohost Gayle King, Clarkson shared that she never expected to become a pop star. "I just wanted to sing," she admitted. "And my initial goal actually even when I was little, wasn't to be the frontrunner. I wanted to be a backup singer. I am so happy we have Madonna, and Britney and Beyoncé—ya'll just live it up. I wanna be, like, right underneath."[5] Whether she envisioned it or not, she became one of the most successful artists of the new century, with multiple hit songs in the years that followed her *American Idol* win.

> **"I just wanted to sing. And my initial goal actually even when I was little, wasn't to be the frontrunner. I wanted to be a backup singer. I am so happy we have Madonna, and Britney and Beyoncé—ya'll just live it up. I wanna be, like, right underneath."[5]**
>
> —Kelly Clarkson, 2013

The show, too, went on to become a pop culture icon. It ran for fifteen consecutive seasons, producing some of the biggest names in music today. To date, its most successful winner is Carrie Underwood, who appeared in the show's fourth season. In addition to her impressive record sales, the country artist has amassed numerous awards for her work, including seven Grammys. Some of the biggest stars to come from the show actually did not win, however. Jennifer Hudson came in seventh in 2004, but she has gone on to win a Grammy and an Oscar. Adam Lambert also did not win his season of *American Idol*, but he went on to become the first openly gay artist to debut at the top of the Billboard charts. After leaving the Fox network in 2016, the show returned to the air on ABC in 2017. The show's success has led to many other televised talent shows, such as *The Voice* and *America's Got Talent*. In 2017, Hudson joined *The Voice* as a coach. A year later, Clarkson also joined the show's coaching team. Brynn Cartelli, a singer Clarkson mentored, became the champion of season fourteen.

# New Century, New Media

During the twentieth century, a record deal was the mark of a singer's big break. Just being able to record in a professional studio with the latest audio equipment was an elusive goal for most performers. Studio time cost a small fortune. Most aspiring artists lacked the money to invest in a demo record to help them get discovered. For established artists, albums were the bread and butter of their musical careers. Selling records is what made musicians both rich and famous. By 2000, vinyl records, which had been the dominant music format in the mid-twentieth century, had largely become a thing of the past. Cassette tapes, popular in the 1970s and 1980s, had also mostly vanished. CDs were the most popular format for buying music at the dawn of the twenty-first century. But new technology was beginning to change the music industry.

Advancing computer technology in the late 1990s and early 2000s meant that audio files could be recorded in a digital format called MP3. This format made sharing songs—or entire albums—especially easy. Websites and services soon allowed users to send MP3 files

Napster helped change the music industry. Though it only lasted a few years before being shut down, it helped lead to the digital music revolution.

to one another and download songs for free. A computer coder named Shawn Fanning created a program called Napster in 1999 that made this practice of music sharing explode. He made Napster freely available to the public, and by March 2000, Napster had more than 20 million users worldwide. By summer, these users were downloading an average of 14,000 songs each minute.

As many artists and their labels feared, record sales around the globe began to slow. Some people had little sympathy over superstars or highly paid executives losing a small amount of their potential income—after all, these people would still make millions of dollars despite this new service. Others pointed out that it wasn't just the wealthiest people in the business who would suffer from free music sharing. Creating albums involves a wide range of workers, many of whom make much more modest salaries. Backup musicians and singers, technicians who adjust the recordings to make them sound as perfect as possible, and even the artists who design the covers for CDs all depended on record sales to make their living.

The law, however, was on the side of the creators and the copyright holders. Downloading an artist's music without the consent of that artist or the record label violated copyright laws. The Record Industry Association of America (RIAA) sued Napster, as did some of the music artists themselves. In February 2001, a judge hearing the RIAA's case ruled that file sharing was a breach of copyright law. The judgment officially instructed Napster to start charging for the service it was providing or put an end to it altogether.

## Downloads and Streaming

Napster's rise and fall may have taken only a couple of years, but the service had permanently changed the way people consumed music. Fans liked the idea of being able to obtain music so quickly from the comfort of their own homes. The problem with Napster was the illegality of its business model, not the fact that it used modern computer technology.

Apple Computer, under the leadership of chief executive officer Steve Jobs, believed it had a solution that would make both the entertainment industry and music fans happy. In 2001, the company launched a new product called the iPod. This portable digital music player let users store a thousand songs in their pocket. Users could copy songs from CDs they owned onto their computers, allowing them to build up a large digital music library. A few years later, in 2003,

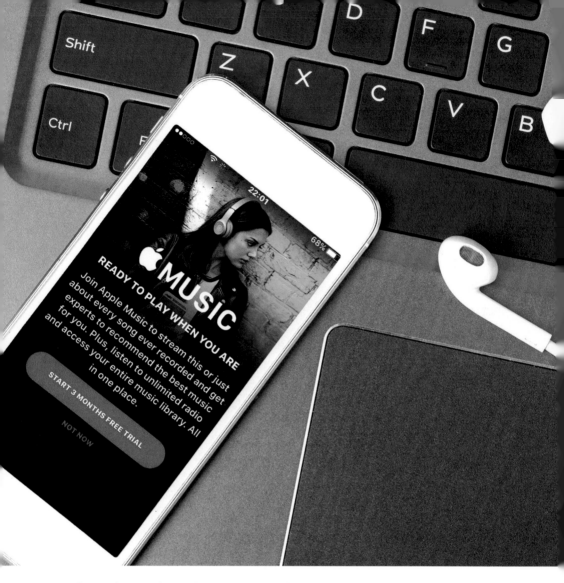

Streaming music services such as Apple Music helped create a new shift in the music industry. Rather than owning their music, many users simply paid monthly fees to access a streaming service's whole catalog.

Apple launched the iTunes Music Store. Now, users could legally buy digital music and listen to it on their computers or iPods. For the first time, users could buy individual songs that they liked, rather than having to purchase a whole album. The iTunes Music Store passed 1 billion downloads in 2006. In 2013, the 25 billionth song was sold on the store.

By the 2010s, Apple and other companies, including Pandora and Spotify, began to offer a different model of music service. Rather than selling individual songs and albums, these new services charged users a set fee per month. In exchange for that fee, users could stream an unlimited amount of music from the service's catalog. Subscriptions to these services are once again shifting the way people listen to music. A 2016 article in the *Harvard Business Review* discussed how this might change the music industry: "This shift has the potential to reshape both the music people listen to and the music that artists create. For example, will the concept of albums survive in the age of streaming, or will artists simply release their best singles?"[6]

Not everyone has jumped on the streaming bandwagon. A smaller yet sizeable part of the population in the twenty-first century has decided to embrace vinyl albums once again. Interest in these old-fashioned records has in fact been strong enough to prompt a number of artists to release new music in this format as well. Although one might assume that it's nostalgic older generations who are responsible for this resurgence, it is actually people aged eighteen to twenty-four who are bringing vinyl back. According to *Forbes* magazine, one in four people in this age range bought a vinyl record in 2017. Some like the way vinyl records sound, while others prefer the ritual of placing a record on a turntable over simply hitting "play" on a computer.

## Beyoncé Thrives as a Solo Artist

It would be impossible to select just one artist who defines the music of the twenty-first century, but if one were to make a list of the top contenders, Beyoncé would surely be on it. During her time as a member of the R&B trio Destiny's Child, Beyoncé Knowles launched her solo career in 2003. She debuted at the top spot on the Billboard 200, propelling her newfound status as an individual performer with a single-word name.

Beyoncé later decided to leave Destiny's Child behind and move on to additional solo projects. Many performers strike out on their own to prove their worth as individuals and artists, but this wasn't the case for Beyoncé. "I'd say I discovered my power after the first Destiny's Child album," she has said. "The label didn't really believe we were pop stars. They underestimated us, and because of that, they allowed us to write our own songs and write our own video treatments. It ended up being the best thing, because that's when I became an artist and took control."[7]

Beyoncé's personal life has also put her in the pop culture spotlight. Married to rap performer and producer Jay-Z since 2008, she now has three children. Their daughter, Blue Ivy, arrived in 2012, with twin siblings Rumi and Sir arriving in 2017. To announce her pregnancy with the twins in February of that year, Beyoncé posted a photo of herself on Instagram. The image showed the expecting mother kneeling in front of a display of colorful flowers, looking at the camera through a veil, and gently holding her belly. With more than 11 million likes, the image became the most-liked post on the social media platform that year.

In 2016, Beyoncé performed a highly praised halftime show at Super Bowl 50 with fellow music artists Coldplay and Bruno Mars. The appearance was not without controversy, however, as the artist used the opportunity to make a profound statement. She performed her new single "Formation," which addressed injustices African Americans face around the United States. Beyoncé had released a bold video for the song the previous day. Vox's Caroline Framke wrote that the video, "proudly steeped in black American culture, celebrates black femininity, and is overtly political, with Beyoncé sinking a New Orleans cop car as a little boy in a hoodie dances in front of riot cops."[8] Even more than when she left Destiny's Child, Beyoncé was taking control of her voice as a performer and artist.

# Justin Bieber Finds an Audience Online

Taking control as artists has become much easier in the twenty-first century, thanks to advancing technology. Just as digital music has made it easier for fans to purchase music, computers and the internet have also made it easier for aspiring artists to find their audience.

## Surprise Album Releases

The most devoted fans anxiously await the releases of their favorite artists' new albums. Knowing this, marketing departments typically plan these releases carefully. They utilize multiple forms of advertising, promote contests and giveaways, and even schedule appearances during which the artists perform certain songs as teasers. Or at least this is the way album releases used to happen. In the twenty-first century, a new method has emerged—dropping albums with absolutely no notice.

Beyoncé was at the center of this defining trend. Instead of following the standard rules of how to release an album, she decided to surprise her fans by dropping a self-titled album in December 2013. It included fourteen new songs and seventeen videos. She called it her first "visual album." Many other artists have followed her lead, dropping albums of their own as surprises for their fans. It has proved to be a fun and effective means of drawing immediate attention to the music. It also keeps the fans on their toes, always looking to see what may have come out on a particular day with no notice.

In 2006, twelve-year-old Justin Bieber was much like any other boy his age—except for his impressive musical ability. Bieber began uploading videos of himself competing in school talent shows in his native Ontario, Canada. He quickly noticed his total views skyrocketing from hundreds to tens of thousands.

One of the people watching was Scooter Braun, a marketing executive who wanted to manage the young artist. He encouraged Bieber to keep posting his videos to lay the groundwork for his future career. "Justin is truly talented," explained Braun in a 2011 interview. "He is that special superstar that you see once in a lifetime. He plays four instruments, self-taught. He showed that in his YouTube channel. He had an incredible tone in his voice. He was captivating and I think that the marketing was right. At the end of the day, the secret to the marketing was to keep it organic and authentic."[9]

Audiences responded to this strategy. Thousands of young girls bought Bieber's music along with tickets to his concerts, where they screamed his name in unison. Adults likened the phenomenon to the way teenaged girls had responded to the Beatles when they first arrived in the United States in the 1960s. Instead of "Beatlemania," the press called it

> **"Justin is truly talented. He is that special superstar that you see once in a lifetime. He plays four instruments, self-taught. He showed that in his YouTube channel. He had an incredible tone in his voice. He was captivating and I think that the marketing was right. At the end of the day, the secret to the marketing was to keep it organic and authentic."[9]**
>
> —Scooter Braun, speaking of Justin Bieber, 2011

"Bieber Fever."[10] The reaction had all the makings of a passing fad, but that is exactly what Bieber didn't want to become. As he explained in an interview on the *Today* show, "I want to have longevity, have my fans grow with me, and not just be a teen artist but kind of move up and be an adult artist."[11] His continued success in the coming years would grant that wish and then some. In 2017, he became the first artist in history to have the three best-selling songs on Billboard's music charts at the same time.

YouTube has also become a powerful vehicle for other musical talent in the twenty-first century. Alessia Cara started her YouTube channel in 2010 when she was just 16. Two years later it had more than 31,000 subscribers when a talent scout at Republic Records discovered the singer. Comedienne and talk show host Ellen DeGeneres gave Charlie Puth his start after seeing a video of a song he uploaded when he was a student at Berklee College of Music. Shawn Mendes utilized YouTube as a stepping stone in a different way. He learned how to play the guitar by watching videos on the platform—and went on to get discovered by posting videos of himself performing to the social media app Vine.

# The Passing of the King of Pop

As new artists were making their way onto the pop music scene, the genre's king, Michael Jackson, reached a sad and sudden end to his illustrious career and life. On June 25, 2009, an ambulance pulled into the driveway at Jackson's Beverly Hills home. The paramedics had received a call regarding a fifty-year-old male in apparent cardiac arrest. What those paramedics did not know until they arrived at the scene was that the patient was one of the most famous musicians of all time.

Although the emergency crew rushed Jackson to the hospital, the doctors there were unable to resuscitate him. He died at 2:26 p.m. Fans across the world were heartbroken, in shock over the loss of a man who had dominated the music charts for an impressive portion of his life. He had begun his career at just five years old with the Jackson 5, a group comprised of Michael and his four older brothers, but it was his solo career that would earn him the title "the King of Pop" from his many fans. Now his fans swarmed outside his home and the hospital, visibly shaken over the news of his passing.

Jackson's death was later revealed to be the result of a fatal combination of medications prescribed to him by his personal physician, Dr. Conrad Murray. Jackson had asked for medication to help him sleep, but the doctor gave him what a court later determined to be an excessive amount of the drug propofol. Murray was subsequently convicted of manslaughter in Jackson's death. Although the pop star is gone, his music lives on in the twenty-first century, entertaining fans and inspiring new artists who still consider him to be pop royalty.

## Kanye West Attracts Controversy

By 2009, Taylor Swift had already made a name for herself as one of the most successful crossover artists in history, but she was eager to be recognized for her hard work. When she won the award for Best Female Video at the MTV Video Music Awards (VMAs) for her video for her hit song "You Belong with Me," she walked to the stage, ready to deliver her acceptance speech. But suddenly, she was interrupted by another artist. In a move no one saw coming, acclaimed rap star Kanye West stormed the stage, commandeering the microphone and the moment from Swift. He assured her that he would let her finish

Kanye West became one of the twenty-first century's most popular rappers. He received critical acclaim for his music, and he also attracted attention for his off-stage behavior.

her speech, and then shared his opinion about who had deserved to win the category. Shocked and obviously disappointed by Swift's victory, he told the audience, "Beyoncé had one of the best videos of all time!"[12]

West soon apologized for his move, but in 2013, he seemed unapologetic. He told the *New York Times*, "I don't have one regret. If anyone's reading this waiting for some type of full-on, flat apology for anything, they should just stop reading right now."[13] The media continues to keep tabs on the relationship between the two artists, watching them closely whenever they show up at the same events or places. Although the incident will forever be a part of West's legacy, he has continued to impress music fans with his work while also being criticized for his sometimes-eccentric behavior. He is one of the best-selling rap artists in history.

West married reality television star Kim Kardashian in 2014, and the couple has been in the news for one reason or another practically ever since. West continually surprises the press, whether he's fervently supporting President Donald Trump or suggesting that he will run for the highest office in the United States himself. Perhaps even more than his talent as a rap musician, what he is best known for is his self-admitted large ego. Whether other people love or hate him, West clearly has a confident view of himself. During his *VH1 Storytellers* show, he said frankly, "My greatest pain in life is that I will never be able to see myself perform live."[14]

## Lady Gaga: Style and Substance

Unusual behavior actually isn't all that unusual for many music artists. Some musicians are eccentric by nature; others appear to work at creating a unique brand to help them stand out from the crowd. In 2010, Lady Gaga wore a dress made entirely of meat to the VMAs. During an appearance on Ellen DeGeneres's talk show, *Ellen*, the music artist explained why she chose this unconventional outfit. "It has many interpretations," she said, "but for me this evening it's [saying], 'If we don't stand up for what we believe in, if we don't fight for our rights, pretty soon we're going to have as much rights as the meat on our bones.'"[15]

In later years, Lady Gaga shifted away from much of this shock value and put her musical talent up front. In 2018, she even ventured into the realm of acting when she took on the leading role in a remake of *A Star Is Born*, the movie made famous by Barbra Streisand in 1976. Released on October 5, it topped $100 million at the box office after just a few weeks. *Forbes* called it "essentially the third-biggest live-action musical over the last 44 years."[16] Lady Gaga no longer needed publicity stunts to get people's attention.

> **"It has many interpretations, but for me this evening it's [saying], 'If we don't stand up for what we believe in, if we don't fight for our rights, pretty soon we're going to have as much rights as the meat on our bones.'"[15]**
>
> —*Lady Gaga, about the meat dress she wore to 2010 MTV Video Music Awards*

Other music artists of the twenty-first century have taken extreme measures to protect their identities. Guy-Manuel de Homem-Christo and Thomas Bangalter are better known as the musical duo Daft Punk, but one thing that is not well known about them is their appearance. Both men wear opaque helmets that make them resemble robots. For a long time, the singer Sia used her hair to disguise her own face. Being in the spotlight of pop culture can be a lot of pressure, so artists like these may choose to seek out such forms of anonymity.

# Chapter 2

# Television and Movies in the Twenty-First Century

The same trend that brought *American Idol* into living rooms across the country at the beginning of the twenty-first century also brought other types of reality television to the mainstream. The shows were not only popular but were also cheaper to produce than scripted comedies or dramas. One of the first shows to capture the attention of the American public was *Survivor*. This show, which challenged its contestants to outwit, outplay, and outlast their competitors in a remote location with few supplies, premiered in May 2000. It was unlike anything previously seen on television. The players, who were assigned to one of two tribes, were ordinary people from all walks of life. Each one had to survive in this wild environment while formulating a strategy to snag the highly coveted $1 million prize.

Like *American Idol*, *Survivor* eliminated a contestant each week the show aired, but unlike the singing competition, this show left the decision of who would be leaving up to the person's fellow tribe members. The competitors soon realized that the best way to move through the game was to create alliances with other players, but knowing whom to trust was tricky. No matter how loyal people seemed, they could still turn on their supposed allies.

Jeff Probst has been hosting *Survivor* since the show's debut. He has won several Emmy awards for his work on the show.

One of the most impressive things about *Survivor* has been its longevity. In September 2018, the thirty-seventh group of castaways began their harsh journey on the show. *Survivor* host Jeff Probst offered his opinion about why the show has continued to thrive for so long during a 2013 interview with the *Globe and Mail*. "Ultimately," he said, "the success of the show is about seeing all of these vastly different personalities interact."[17] That success has also inspired many other types of reality television. *The Amazing Race*, *The Great British Baking Show*, and *Dancing with the Stars* are just a few of the other reality programs that have developed dedicated followings in the twenty-first century.

Not only have viewers been entertained by these shows, but they have also been inspired by them. The effects can even be seen in the world economy. *The Great British Baking Show*, known outside the United Kingdom as *The Great British Bake Off*, triggered an increase in the sales of the appliances and supplies used on the show. Richard Williams owns Williams Supermarket in Somerset, England. In a 2015 interview with Chartered Management Institute, he shared, "Home-baking is already popular here and it does tend to rise in the weeks during and after *The Great British Bake Off* . . ."[18] Similarly, *Who Do You Think You Are?*, a show that reveals the family history of a different celebrity each week, has prompted people all over the world to add genealogy to their list of hobbies.

# Medical Marvels

Dramatic television shows that take place in hospitals have become increasingly popular in the twenty-first century. Still, when *Grey's Anatomy* premiered in 2005, few would have expected it to still be on the air—and still receiving high ratings—15 years later. What has surprised viewers even more, however, has been the show's continual ability to tackle social issues with both dramatic flair and unparalleled sensitivity. The result has created an audience that eagerly tunes in each week to see what will happen next at Grey-Sloan Memorial Hospital.

Years before same-sex marriage was legal throughout the United States, *Grey's Anatomy* featured the wedding of a same-sex couple. The marriage was far from the only storyline for doctors Callie Torres and Arizona Robbins, which may have been why the show's depiction of the lesbian couple felt so authentic to fans. Their sexuality was just one aspect of these multidimensional characters. In another storyline, a mass shooting took place at the hospital, a type of tragedy that has been in real-life headlines frequently in the 2010s. The show also tackled the topic of racial bias when a police officer shot and killed an African American teen entering his home through a window after forgetting his house keys. The episode ended with Grey-Sloan's chief of surgery having what she called "the talk" with her own child, explaining to him that he would be held to a higher standard than his white friends in any situation with the police. "Your only goal is to get home safely," Chief Miranda Bailey tells her thirteen-year-old son.[19]

## Hannah Montana

In 2006, a television sitcom called *Hannah Montana* premiered on the Disney Channel. The show's main character, Miley Stewart, was a typical middle school student beset by the typical array of problems faced by thirteen-year-old girls in the twenty-first century. What wasn't typical about Stewart, however, was that she kept a very big secret. At night she performed as one of the most popular singers in pop music—Hannah Montana. The show was an instant hit with young people, to whom the idea of living such an exciting double life seemed thrilling.

Miley Cyrus's career became even bigger after *Hannah Montana* ended. She gained attention for her catchy songs and her over-the-top performances.

The program's success was also the result of the obvious talent of its young star, Miley Cyrus, the daughter of country musician Billy Ray Cyrus. Michael Poryes, the show's executive producer, told *Time*, "In Miley we found the perfect girl to carry off this part. She has a kind of strength and sweetness that make her character appealing, an unmistakable something that makes you believe she's a star."[20] And a star is exactly what Cyrus became. As the show's popularity kept building, so did the star's own career. Eventually, it led to a *Hannah*

*Montana* movie and finally a musical career for Cyrus that grew far beyond the Disney character.

At first Cyrus found the tween image difficult to break from, and as she became a young adult, she began doing some extreme things to separate herself from the squeaky-clean image that had made her famous. Although many fans stuck by her during this time, others worried that she was taking things too far. Drugs, sex, and shock value had become integral aspects of her new image. Her more scandalous performances often included twerking and sticking out her tongue in sexually suggestive ways that made parents of her fans highly concerned about her new image. Although *Hannah Montana* had ended production in 2011, many people felt that Cyrus was a role model for young girls, and they felt she was acting irresponsibly.

In time Cyrus developed an older fan base, which included many of the young adults who had grown up with her. She kept acting, making films such as *The Last Song* and *LOL*, but music has remained a significant part of her life. At 24, she also made the decision to give up alcohol and drugs. "I want to be super clear and sharp," she told *Billboard*, "because I know exactly where I want to be."[21]

## Women in the White House

The century began with President Bill Clinton in the White House and another Democrat, this one fictional, serving as president on a show called *The West Wing*. Martin Sheen played President Jed Bartlet on the NBC political drama, which was one of the most popular programs on television during its seven-year run.

More recently, several actresses have stepped into the role of a female president on the small screen—including Bellamy Young on

*Scandal*, Julia Louis-Dreyfus on *Veep*, and most recently Robin Wright on *House of Cards*. In a 2014 article in *Vogue* magazine, culture writer Patricia Garcia explained, "In the past decade or so, women have made some impressive gains in the political sphere. We've had three female Secretaries of State since 1997, our first female Speaker of the House of Representatives, three women on the current Supreme Court, and after this month's mid-term elections, a record-breaking more than 100 women in the next Congress. As women take over our ballots, isn't it only logical they take over our TV screens too?"[22]

## Big Laughs

In 2007, a sitcom about socially awkward physicist Sheldon Cooper and his three friends premiered on CBS. Much of the humor was provided courtesy of Penny, a peppy young blonde woman who moves in across the hall during the first episode. An aspiring actress, Penny does not always understand her new neighbors, but that doesn't keep her from trying. The combination of the nerdy scientists and the aspiring actress set the scene for the sitcom's humorous situations.

The enormous success of *The Big Bang Theory* was a prime example of art imitating life. So-called geek culture was at an all-time high when the show began, likely part of the reason that viewers embraced Sheldon, Leonard, Howard, and Raj so enthusiastically. Like many real young men of the twenty-first century, they read comic books, attended superhero movies, and passionately collected memorabilia related to both.

Despite its success, however, the show had its share of critics. Many people who proudly identified as nerds thought that the show perpetuated stereotypes of geeky pastimes and the people who enjoy them. But in time *The Big Bang Theory* even won over some of its critics. Writer Craig Byrne told the *Today* show, "When I first saw the show, I admit I found it to be a little bit overdone. But then I realized that the fact that it's grossly overdone is what makes it funny."[23]

## Zombies Everywhere

On Halloween night in 2010, a television show called *The Walking Dead* aired its first episode on the AMC network. Its premise was a bit outlandish. A virus has led to the death of millions of human beings, who simultaneously developed an ability to keep walking despite their demise and a nasty hunger for human flesh. The zombies, dubbed walkers by the show's living characters, are the show's first antagonists, but over several seasons a bigger threat to human safety emerges—the living. In this horrific new world, laws are no longer enforced. People must sometimes do some unimaginable things to survive, and this chaos has pushed them to the edge of their humanity.

*The Walking Dead* helped make zombies a pop culture phenomenon. Zombies could soon be found everywhere, from Halloween costumes to toys to movies to video games.

The concept of zombies was not a new one, but the overnight success of this program about them was unprecedented. In 2016, not even *Sunday Night Football* could compete with the show's ratings on the night of its seventh season premiere. One of the reasons fans tuned in was that it seemed like anything could happen. The show had a tendency to kill off popular characters with little to no warning. In other TV shows, disasters may strike frequently, but the viewers can typically count on the stars making it through whatever turmoil they face. In the constantly changing setting of *The Walking Dead*, however, no character seemed to be safe.

While some characters have been more popular than others, it is often the relationships between various members of the ensemble that appeal most to fans. Many of the cast members have an uncanny chemistry with one another. Lauren Cohan, who plays the character Maggie, shared in *Interview* magazine that each time a character is killed off, the whole group gets together for a farewell meal. "We always have these death dinners," she said, "and we've obviously had so many people leave now. We still have the really sad part of the night where everyone sort of says their goodbyes, but Danai [Gurira, who plays Michonne] had this great idea to liven it up for the second part. We finished the night singing Backstreet Boys karaoke and everything else cheesy you can imagine."[24]

## Reboots and Remakes

Nostalgia for television of the past has led to several revivals of old shows. These are commonly known as reboots. Some of the most popular programs of the last few decades have returned to television in the twenty-first century, extending their storylines and giving audiences more time with characters they enjoyed in the past. *Murphy Brown*, *Will & Grace*, and *Gilmore Girls* attracted huge fan bases in the 1980s, 1990s, and 2000s, respectively. In the 2010s, the casts of these shows went back to work, giving their characters an unexpected second life.

Debra Messing, who plays the female lead in *Will & Grace*, thinks that this reboot has been met with such a great reception because the show has remained timely while holding onto its unique mixture of candor and fun. As the actress pointed out in a 2017 interview in

*Vanity Fair*, "The show from the very beginning always shone a light on hypocrisy or questionable things that are happening within our culture—whether it's pop culture, whether it's politics—and you know it was always done in a way that was sassy. And would inspire a belly laugh."[25]

Another rapidly growing trend has been remakes of popular shows. These new programs have similar titles and premises to their older versions, but with new casts and other twists. *Fuller House*, *One Day at a Time*, and *Queer Eye* have all enjoyed great success

## Cutting Those Cords

The way people watch television and movies has changed dramatically during the twenty-first century. As media transitioned from VHS tapes to DVDs, a new company emerged to make movie viewing easier. Netflix offered an extensive library of movies and TV programs on DVD, which they mailed to customers who subscribed to their innovative new service. For a monthly fee, they could exchange movies continually, sending them back to the company in convenient prepaid envelopes. Soon, video stores, which had dominated the home video market in the previous two decades, were closing in increasing numbers. Subscription services were now the new standard.

As time and technology moved forward, streaming video also became an option—one that Netflix steered its customers toward. Instead of having to wait for a disc to arrive in the mail, people could watch movies instantly over the internet. Other companies, such as Hulu and Amazon, have also jumped on the streaming bandwagon, making it easy to watch films—or binge entire television seasons—at a moment's notice. Streaming led many people to see cable television as obsolete. So-called "cord cutters" cancel their cable service and use streaming subscriptions to watch most of their television programs.

with a mixture of their original fans and new audiences. This trend has also carried over to the big screen with remakes of movies such as *Flatliners*, *Ocean's Eleven*, and *True Grit*. Fans and critics alike have argued that some of these television and film remakes have been even better than the originals.

# The *Star Wars* Saga

While the most recent *Star Wars* films have not been remakes, the space fantasy saga's resurgence in the twenty-first century also sprang from nostalgia for a phenomenon of the past. The first movie, *Star Wars*, premiered in 1977, followed closely by two sequels. Many of the fans who first saw these films as children returned to the theaters as adults when three prequels were released between 1999 and 2005. The first of these movies, *Star Wars Episode I: The Phantom Menace*, earned $924 million worldwide, and it introduced a whole new generation to the series' universe.

Diehard fans of the original Star Wars films were critical of the prequels. In its review of 2002's *Star Wars Episode II: Attack of the Clones*, *Rolling Stone* called *The Phantom Menace* "a prequel that everyone saw and no one wants to remember."[26] None of the poor reviews or bad word of mouth diminished the desire of moviegoers to flock to theaters once again in 2015 when the first film in a new trilogy, *Star Wars Episode VII: The Force Awakens*, hit theaters. The film raked in $1 billion in its first twelve days.

# Putting Wakanda on the Map

In 2018, a superhero movie unlike any other hit the theaters. In some ways it was similar to other popular films about people with

Fans continue to crave new entries in the *Star Wars* saga. The new movies released in the early twenty-first century all became box-office hits.

superpowers. Its main character, T'Challa, had incredible speed, stamina, and strength. What made this superhero, played by Chadwick Boseman, stand out most among all others, however, was the fact that he represented a group of people who until this point had seen few superheroes who looked like them. T'Challa and nearly all the other characters in *Black Panther* were of African descent.

The film, set in the fictional African nation of Wakanda, was an instant hit. It made $242 million in the United States during its opening four-day weekend leading up to President's Day. Excitement and pride over the first black superhero on the big screen inspired numerous celebrities to sponsor free screenings for underprivileged kids whose parents could not afford the cost of the tickets. Kendrick Lamar, who performed music on the movie's soundtrack, treated children from three housing projects in Los Angeles, California, to the film. Actress and singer Zendaya took kids to a theater in her hometown of Oakland, California. Rap artist Tee Grizzley held a private screening for public school kids in his birthplace of Detroit, Michigan. He told the *Detroit News*, "I'm excited to share this opportunity with students from my city. I have to give back to the community that raised and made me. This is bigger than a movie; it's about investing in our own."[27]

## An Incredible Reception

In the 2010s, the superhero movie became a dominant genre. Characters such as Iron Man, Batman, and Captain America starred in smash hit films. One reason for this success is that kids and adults alike often enjoy a good superhero movie. In 2004, the superhero phenomenon had barely started to emerge when the computer animation company Pixar released a film about a family of superheroes called *The Incredibles*. Each member of the Parr family had a special gift. At home, Mr. and Mrs. Parr were like any other parents, encouraging their kids Violet and Dash to do their homework and eat their vegetables.

> **"I'm excited to share this opportunity with students from my city. I have to give back to the community that raised and made me. This is bigger than a movie; it's about investing in our own."[27]**
>
> —Tee Grizzley on the private screening of Black Panther he held for school kids in Detroit, 2018

But whenever danger arose in their hometown of Metroville, they donned masks and fought crime as the super-strong Mr. Incredible and mind-bendingly flexible Elastigirl. Violet's ability to create force fields and Dash's exceptional speed also came in handy, even though their parents did not approve of the kids placing themselves in harm's way. The result was a superhero story that families could enjoy together.

Audiences couldn't wait for a sequel to the popular flick, but waiting was exactly what they had to do—for fourteen years. While other Pixar films, such as *Toy Story* and *Cars*, had successful sequels during this period, *The Incredibles* did not, despite obvious demand. Some people suspected that if Pixar waited too long to release a second movie, it would not be nearly as successful as other follow-up films had been. What if by the time the second movie was made, fans had forgotten the first one?

> **"You don't get to this level of opening without appealing to everyone, whether you're a fan of animation, superheroes, or just out to have a good time and want to see a good movie."[28]**
>
> — *Walt Disney Studios executive Cathleen Taff, regarding the enthusiastic reception for* Incredibles 2, *2018*

Any fears of this kind were proven wrong in 2018 when the highly anticipated *Incredibles 2* finally had its opening day in June. Parents once again crowded theaters along with their kids to see the latest installment about the extraordinary lives of the Parrs. During its opening weekend, the movie grossed $180 million. It was the biggest box office reception ever for an animated film.

What was most surprising about the long lines at theaters to see the new movie, though, was

*Incredibles 2* became a massive hit. Even fourteen years after the previous movie, fans were excited to see the characters and where they were going next.

the lack of children in many of these groups. Adults without kids made up nearly one-third of the ticket buyers. Cathleen Taff, head of distribution for Walt Disney Studios, saw the broad reception as a direct result of how versatile the film was. As she explained to *USA Today*, "You don't get to this level of opening without appealing to everyone, whether you're a fan of animation, superheroes, or just out to have a good time and want to see a good movie."[28]

# Chapter 3

# Popular Books of the Twenty-First Century

In May 2018, a new television series premiered on PBS. Called *The Great American Read*, the show was a competition for selecting America's most-loved novel. Over a period of nearly five months, viewers voted for their favorite books. By September, more than 2 million people had cast votes. They could vote as many times as they wanted, but only once per day. The top 100 titles varied wildly in subject matter, setting, and genre. Many of the books had been written decades earlier, and some more than a century ago. But what the novels all shared was an ongoing popularity in the twenty-first century.

Audiences showed immediate interest in the competition in more ways than one. In addition to voting for their favorites, readers sought out other books on the list. At least one author in the running for the number one spot even sang the praises of the other books. James Patterson, who was nominated for his Alex Cross mystery series, told *USA Today* that he planned to vote for the *Harry Potter* series by J.K. Rowling. These books star a young wizard named Harry Potter who attends a magical school. Calling the series great, Patterson added that it had done a great deal of good for the world. "Any kid who read all the 'Harry Potters,' or even one of them, is now a competent reader. That's just so essential. And creating competent readers in this country saves lives. J.K. Rowling has saved thousands and thousands of lives in this country and around the world."[29]

Patterson clearly isn't the only person who feels passionate about Rowling's books. After all the votes in *The Great American Read* were tallied, the *Harry Potter* series placed third in the competition. Only *To Kill a Mockingbird* by Harper Lee and Diana Gabaldon's *Outlander* series placed higher, taking first and second respectively. Rowling had indeed changed the way kids perceived books. In an age when most kids seemed to prefer television, computers, and video games over books, Harry Potter brought young people back to the printed word in droves. The series has sold more than 500 million books in seventy-three languages.

Rowling also had a significant impact on other children's books. Prior to the release of the first Harry Potter book, publishers were not hopeful for the sales of most children's novels. They simply weren't selling as well as they had in the past. Following Rowling's gargantuan success, publishers increased the number of children's titles they released. The length of many children's books also increased, a trend many people in the business linked to Rowling, whose books were known

> **"Any kid who read all the 'Harry Potters,' or even one of them, is now a competent reader. That's just so essential. And creating competent readers in this country saves lives. J.K. Rowling has saved thousands and thousands of lives in this country and around the world."[29]**
>
> —Author James Patterson, 2018

Rowling's *Harry Potter* series helped inspire a generation to read. The series later spawned movies, toys, and even a theme park.

for their impressive thickness. A year before the first *Harry Potter* novel was released, the average book for a child between eight and twelve was about 140 pages long. By 2016, the average book for this demographic was more than twice as long. Adults, too, embraced the *Harry Potter* series, whether reading the books to their children or attending midnight book release parties on their own. The accompanying movie franchise was also a huge success with people of all ages.

# A Song of Ice and Fire

Like *Harry Potter,* George R.R. Martin's *A Song of Ice and Fire* book series began in the 1990s, but it became more popular during the twenty-first century. Martin has admitted that following the publication of the first novel, *A Game of Thrones*, he even had a book signing in Saint Louis, Missouri, to which not even a single fan showed up. Still, the book sold enough copies to continue the series. The publisher had originally bought the story as a trilogy, but Martin soon realized that he needed more space to finish the intricate tale he had begun weaving. The publisher was thrilled to hear this, because by this time the novels were selling in record numbers. HBO had even developed an enormously popular television adaptation, *Game of Thrones*, as a result of the books' success. To date Martin has sold more than 70 million books, and the series has been translated into more than forty languages.

Martin quickly gained a reputation as a prolific killer of his own characters. Major characters are sometimes killed off without warning, leaving audiences thinking that no one in the books is safe. Martin is also known for taking his time with his writing. By 2018 he had published five books in the series and had plans for two more. The sixth book had been in the works for several years, with several planned release dates coming and going. The plot of the television series passed the point it had reached in the fifth book, taking the storyline into uncharted territory. No one but Martin himself knows exactly when he will finish his saga.

Certainly, writing such a complex story takes a great deal of time. Unlike most novels, Martin's books do not have a single protagonist. Instead, he tells the story through the eyes of many different characters, rather than focusing on a single lead character. Another thing that makes Martin's series stand out from most other

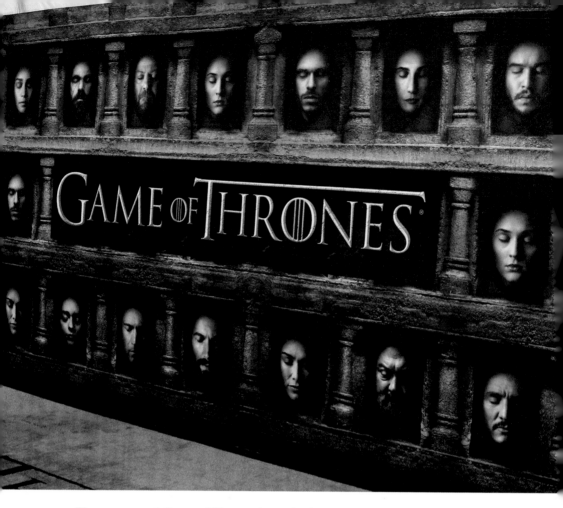

The success of *Game of Thrones* brought the popularity of Martin's stories to new heights. Each time a new season started, advertising for the show could be seen throughout major cities.

popular fiction is its unique mixture of history and fantasy. The tale is set in the Seven Kingdoms of Westeros, an imaginary place similar in many ways to the Middle Ages of Europe. Just when the reader starts to view the story as realistic historical fiction, however, imaginary creatures such as dragons and undead beings make appearances.

One of the reasons publishers and readers alike are so willing to wait for the next installment in the series is Martin's uncanny ability to write compelling characters and storylines so believably. He also has a knack for challenging readers' perceptions of good and evil. In a

2017 *Time* interview, the author said, "There's this tendency to want to make people into heroes and villains. And I think there are villains in real life and there are heroes in real life. But even the greatest heroes have flaws and do bad things, and even the greatest [villains] are capable of love and pain and occasionally have moments where you can feel sympathetic for them. As much as I love science fiction and fantasy and imaginative stuff, you always have to go back to real life as your touchstone and say, *What is the truth?*"[30]

# Where Science Met Fiction

Mark Watney is on a mission to Mars. He is one of six crew members on the red planet, millions of miles away from Earth, when something goes terribly wrong. The crew scrambles to make an emergency launch to head back home, but in all the commotion, Watney gets left behind with no means of returning to Earth himself. This is how the 2011 novel *The Martian* by Andy Weir begins. Weir hooked readers, inspiring them to keep turning the page until they find out how the botanist-turned-astronaut deals with his interplanetary dilemma.

Weir seemed to be an overnight success, with *The Martian* debuting at number twelve on the *New York Times* bestseller list. But the story of how the book came to stores was much longer than many of his new fans imagined. Weir had worked as a software engineer in Silicon Valley for more than two decades. He had tried his hand at writing fiction, but he couldn't get a publisher or even an agent. When he began the novel that would make him famous, he adjusted his expectations. He didn't stop writing, but he offered his work on his website for his small fan base for free. As he told CNBC in 2017, "By the time I was writing 'The Martian,' it never occurred to me that it was publishable, and I really didn't think it would have any mainstream appeal. I thought I was writing for this tiny little niche audience of one percenter nerds like myself who wanted all the numbers correct and the mathematical proofs in the text."[31]

It turned out that the painstaking scientific details that Weir included in the novel were exactly what mainstream audiences liked about the book. He had started with a seemingly hopeless situation and found a plausible solution, taking the readers along on Watney's harrowing journey. Writing convincing science fiction is challenging, but writing it while relying on technology that actually exists today is something few authors from the genre have done.

Weir's journey to the best seller list began when he listed *The Martian* on Amazon's self-publishing platform. Visitors to his website had asked him to offer the book through Amazon so they could enjoy it on an e-reader. He chose to sell it for just 99 cents because it was the minimum amount he could charge. Readers responded to the offering with great enthusiasm, catapulting the title to the site's list of best-selling science fiction. At this point publishers finally began paying attention to Weir. Soon he had both an agent and movie deal for the novel that has since become a twenty-first century classic.

> **"By the time I was writing 'The Martian,' it never occurred to me that it was publishable, and I really didn't think it would have any mainstream appeal. I thought I was writing for this tiny little niche audience of one percenter nerds like myself who wanted all the numbers correct and the mathematical proofs in the text."[31]**
>
> —Andy Weir, 2017

# A Trek of Self-Discovery

When Cheryl Strayed was just twenty-six years old, she reached a turning point in her life. She had been faced with two very different yet profound losses—the end of her seven-year marriage and the death of her mother, who had passed away four years earlier. Not knowing what she wanted to do next, she decided to put one foot in front of the other, quite literally. She would hike the Pacific Crest Trail, which extends from Southern California to Washington. She wasn't an experienced hiker. In fact, she had never made a backpacking trip in her life. She didn't even know what kind of boots to wear or how much she should carry along the way. Still, none of this stopped her from making a journey from California all the way to Oregon. During

## The Rise of E-Readers

The way that people read books has changed a lot in the twenty-first century. In 2007, Amazon released its first e-reader, the Kindle. Before this time, avid readers had two options for buying the latest best sellers: They could travel to a so-called brick-and-mortar store to purchase their hard copy of the title in question, or they could order the book online and wait for it to arrive in the mail. The Kindle made it possible for readers to browse or search for a specific title and then download the entire book to a wireless device in a matter of seconds.

Since the first Kindle model, several other e-readers have hit the market and sold like hotcakes. Many people especially like being able to store—and travel with—more than 1,000 books on a device at any given time. They can also download samples of books they are considering before they commit to buying the titles—or borrow books from their local libraries. The e-reader phenomenon has become so popular that phones and tablets now offer e-reader apps, making electronic reading a convenient way to devour the written word on all kinds of devices.

the ninety-three days it took her, she rediscovered herself in a way she never expected.

Strayed told the story of her soul-searching journey in her 2012 book *Wild*. The memoir resonated with readers, and particularly with other women who had faced similarly daunting crises in their lives. Hundreds of them traveled to the West Coast to follow in Strayed's footsteps in hopes of recreating her experience. Jessica Reynolds was one such reader. Her mother gave her a copy of the book, which inspired her to start training for the physically intensive endeavor. "It makes your own personal struggles and problems seem so small," she told the *Daily Mail*. "Starting a new life for her was finding herself on this trail and I kind of was in that same point in my life."[32]

Reynolds was wise to train for the hike. When Strayed made her own journey along the trail, her personal discoveries weren't the only unexpected parts of the trip. When she made it to a snow-covered mountain, she realized that she was ill-prepared to cross the imposing land mass. She had none of the gear she needed, making it even more dangerous. She also hadn't anticipated encountering a rattlesnake along her way. At one point Strayed even found herself face-to-face with a bear.

The adventurer wrote in journals along her way, documenting the trip at first for herself and then later turning them into the book that would sell more than 1.3 million

> "I learned so much in those first few years after *Wild* was published about what fame is, how to figure out which opportunities to say yes to and which to decline, and how to stay grounded in my real life, even when crazy glamorous things happen (like getting to attend the Oscars!)."[33]
>
> —Cheryl Strayed, 2018

copies within two years of its publication. The book was also made into a movie starring Reese Witherspoon as Strayed. The fame that came with its success also brought challenges. Strayed told ChasingZest.com, "I learned so much in those first few years after *Wild* was published about what fame is, how to figure out which opportunities to say yes to and which to decline, and how to stay grounded in my real life, even when crazy glamorous things happen (like getting to attend the Oscars!)."[33]

## One Popular Memoir

When Michelle Obama released her memoir, *Becoming*, in November 2018, booksellers suspected it would be a best seller. Obama is a widely beloved former First Lady. Her autobiography ended up becoming the best-selling book of 2018. According to *Publishers Weekly*, the title sold 2 million copies in its first fifteen days on store shelves. Readers purchased 725,000 copies the very first day.

Among the people who sang the book's praises was Oprah Winfrey, who has said she is a big fan of the former First Lady. In an interview for her *O Magazine*, Winfrey asked Obama if she found writing about her personal life difficult. "Actually, no," Obama replied, "because here's the thing that I realized: People always ask me, 'Why is it that you're so authentic?' 'How is it that people connect to you?' And I think it starts because I like me. I like my story and all the bumps and bruises. I think that's what makes me uniquely me. So I've always been open with my staff, with young people, with my friends. And the other thing, Oprah: I know that whether we like it or not, Barack and I are role models."[34]

One of the most common questions that Obama was asked during her book tour for the memoir was whether she was considering

Michelle Obama's popularity as First Lady made her book highly anticipated. She went on a major book tour to promote the memoir in 2018 and 2019.

running for president herself in 2020. Some supporters of her husband's presidency hoped the former First Lady would put her hat in the ring during the next presidential election, but it did not look like their hopes would become a reality. When asked about the likelihood of Mrs. Obama running for this or any political office, Valerie Jarrett, former adviser to President Barack Obama, said, "Let me be very clear, it will never happen."[35]

## Comics Galore!

While comic books have been around for more than a century, these thrilling stories of superheroes have risen to new heights of popularity in the new millennium. The two biggest comic book publishers, Marvel and DC, have also become big names at the box office, which has boosted sales of their graphic novels. Many fans cite the 2000 movie

*X-Men* as prompting the surge of superhero movies. Since then, many comic book heroes have appeared in such smash-hit movies as *The Dark Knight*, *Avengers: Infinity War*, and *Wonder Woman*.

Even television has helped renew interest in comics. *The Walking Dead* began as a comic book and continues to be published in this format. Although the storylines of the comic and the show often diverge, dedicated fans still look to the pages of the comics for clues about what will happen to their favorite characters in future episodes. Many of them actually find the printed medium more exciting. Robert Kirkman, creator of the original *Walking Dead* comic book, also writes for the television series. In an interview with AMC, he shared, "The formats are mostly similar, but the comic book scripts I write are a little more hands-on, more visual direction than a television screen play. . . . When I write a comic book, it's just full steam ahead: I think of something and decide to do it at the same time."[36]

Blockbuster movies and hit TV shows aren't the only factors contributing to the growing interest in this fun art and entertainment form. Pop culture writer Travis M. Andrews explained in an article in the *Washington Post*,

> *For one, comic books are more accessible than ever before, partially because of the internet. Comics, previously purchased at newsstands or in dedicated comic-book stores, can easily be bought and, in some cases, even read digitally—a trend that digital giants have noticed. In 2014, Amazon bought ComiXology, the largest digital comics platform, which sold more than 4 billion pages of comics in 2013.*[37]

One of the things that gives comic books such universal appeal is the diversity of characters seen in the genre. Some of the superheroes, such as Thor, the god of thunder, are rooted in mythology that long predates the history of comic books. Other superheroes, such as Spiderman, are underdogs, overcoming devastating circumstances to develop powers that they had never imagined they could possess. Some heroes, such as Tony Stark and Dr. Stephen Strange, are brilliant minds who often lack humility. This wide range of personalities and backgrounds makes for thrilling storylines.

Comic books have also become increasingly inclusive in recent years. In addition to *Black Panther*'s T'Challa, who has become a major symbol of black representation in comics, the genre also now features female characters who save the day, such *The Walking Dead*'s sword-wielding Michonne. Gay and transsexual characters have also appeared more in twenty-first century comics. Alan Scott, one of the Green Lantern's alter egos, has a boyfriend. And in the *Invisibles* series, Lord Fanny is a trans woman. Comic book artist Neal Adams, who has been working in the industry for many decades, told the *Huffington Post* in 2016, "Times have changed."[38]

Although it is easy to dismiss comic books as adolescent fodder, the twenty-first century has also witnessed a deeper respect for this medium. Dr. Mel Gibson is a comic book expert at Northumbria University in England. In 2013, he told the BBC, "Graphic novels were once seen as throwaway, but now they are more highly valued and viewed as things which deserve space on the bookshelf."[39]

The size and monetary value of some comic book collections show just how seriously some fans take the genre, with diehard enthusiasts often paying jaw-dropping amounts for the rarest volumes. In 2014, an original copy of *Action Comics* #1, which introduced the legendary comic book character Superman in 1938, sold on eBay for $3.2 million. It fetched such a hefty price—the highest ever paid for a comic book at auction—because of the combination of its

A huge variety of comics and graphic novels are available at conventions, at comic book stores, and even on electronic devices. They range from superhero stories to comedies to dramatic narratives on serious subjects.

rarity and pristine condition. Darren Adams, the book's seller, told the *Washington Post*, "I actually held it for a few years—I was so excited about this book. And equally exciting to having a book of this condition is the fact that nobody knew it existed. Most books have a history . . . but this book was totally off the grid and nobody knew about it till I made it known."[40]

# Chapter 4

# Sporting Events That Have Defined the Twenty-First Century

The twenty-first century has marked some historic wins for sports teams that had been waiting a long time for victory—sometimes an extremely long time. One such team was the Chicago Cubs. This team had won the World Series in 1907 and 1908. But the Cubs were later plagued by a supposed curse. This curse was attributed to an angry baseball fan who was denied admission to the fourth game of the 1945 World Series, in which the Cubs were playing against the Detroit Tigers. William Sianis showed up at the gate with two tickets in hand, the first for himself and the second for the goat he had brought to Wrigley Field with him. When the ticket takers refused to allow the animal into the stadium, Sianis responded with threatening words. He told everyone who would listen that the Cubs would not just lose this World Series, but that they also would never win another.

Although the idea of curses may seem farfetched, the Cubs' unsuccessful efforts on the baseball field throughout the next seventy years kept another World Series win out of reach. Over the years the team developed a reputation as one of the worst in Major League Baseball, but whether this was due to lack of skill, poor coaching, or a curse from an angry fan, no one knew for certain. Then, in 2016,

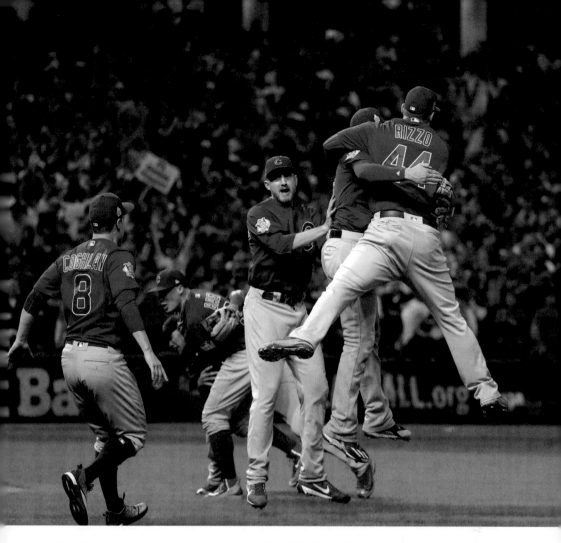

The Cubs were elated when they won the 2016 World Series. It had been more than a century since their last World Series victory.

the Cubs finally achieved the victory that few thought possible. After a stellar regular season, they went on to win the 2016 National League Championship and ultimately the 2016 World Series. Whether the curse had been real or not, it became a thing of the past with the Cubs' thrilling victory against the Cleveland Indians.

Following the historic win, Theo Epstein, president of baseball operations for the Chicago Cubs, reflected on the victory. "I'm just so happy for Cubs fans over the last 108 years, generations, some still here, some not. They were all here tonight. Everybody who's ever

> **"I'm just so happy for Cubs fans over the last 108 years, generations, some still here, some not. They were all here tonight. Everybody who's ever put on a Cubs uniform, this is for you. It took a group of unbelievable men, connected with each other, never quitting. Everyone's prone to hyperbole, but tonight, it was kind of epic, right? It was the way it had to happen."[41]**
>
> —*President of baseball operations for the Chicago Cubs, Theo Epstein, on the team's World Series win in 2016*

put on a Cubs uniform, this is for you. It took a group of unbelievable men, connected with each other, never quitting. Everyone's prone to hyperbole, but tonight, it was kind of epic, right? It was the way it had to happen."[41]

# Brady's Greatest Comeback

While some teams waited decades for a championship title, others were racking them up like there was no tomorrow. In 2017, the NFL's New England Patriots were headed into the Super Bowl to play the championship game against the Atlanta Falcons. It was New England's ninth appearance in football's biggest game. With four wins in the books, Patriots players and fans alike were as confident as ever, but the game didn't go exactly as they had planned.

The Falcons had clearly come to win, taking an early and commanding lead. At one point they led the Patriots 28–3. Many New England fans were preparing for a loss, reminding themselves that four wins since 2002 was nothing to be ashamed of. But then Patriots quarterback Tom Brady began one of the greatest comebacks in sports history. By the time the clock ran out, the score was tied at 28.

The Patriots forced their opponents to go into overtime—something that had never before happened in a Super Bowl. In the end, New England won the game, making Brady the first quarterback to win five Super Bowl rings.

As a veteran of many Super Bowls, Brady knew well that games could quickly head into one team's favor or the other; the end result often depended on mere moments. He also knew that many times

## Believing in Something

Few athletes have inspired more debate in the twenty-first century than Colin Kaepernick. As a quarterback for the San Francisco 49ers, Kaepernick wanted to raise awareness about racism, particularly the incidents of police brutality that many people of color were facing in the United States. To do this, he chose to kneel as the national anthem was played before his football games in 2016.

Reactions from fans were swift and strong. Some saw Kaepernick's refusal to stand as disrespectful to his nation's flag—and by extension to that very nation itself. Others thought that he had chosen a peaceful yet meaningful way to protest the social injustices that seemed to crop up in the news at an alarming rate. In 2017, the 49ers did not opt to renew the quarterback's contract when it expired, leaving him a free agent. Despite his football skills, no other team in the NFL made him an offer. It seemed that Kaepernick's promising football career was over even before he had reached his prime.

His critics were pleased with this outcome, but the public had not seen the last of Kap, as his fans call him. In 2018, Nike released a print ad featuring the former NFL star. The graphic was simple: a close-up black-and-white photo of Kaepernick with text reading, "Believe in something. Even if it means sacrificing everything."

*Quoted in Amir Vera, "How National Anthem Protests Took Colin Kaepernick from Star QB to Unemployment to a Bold Nike Ad," CNN, September 4, 2018. www.cnn.com.*

a team's defense was tired toward the end of the game. Stopping the other team's offense wasn't quite as easy after having already expended so much energy in the earlier quarters. If he and his fellow Patriots could get the ball, he knew they had a shot at winning the game, even with the huge deficit. In an interview with *Sports Illustrated*, Brady said, "We just had to get it to that point, and we had to get ourselves back in the game. And finally at the start of the fourth quarter, I felt like, man we're back in the game."[42]

## James Makes Good on His Promise

The city of Cleveland is famous for several things—its numerous trees, its unusually high volume of lake-effect snow, and being the home of the Rock and Roll Hall of Fame. For many years, though, the city on Ohio's northern border had not been known for a sports championship of any kind—until LeBron James came back to town.

After beginning his professional basketball career playing for the Cleveland Cavaliers straight out of high school in 2003, James went on to megastardom as a forward for the Miami Heat. He won two NBA titles with the Heat in 2012 and 2013. James always said that he would return to Cleveland one day, promising to win a championship for his hometown. After fulfilling the first part of that promise in 2014 when he rejoined the Cavaliers, he went on to lead the team to their long-awaited championship when they won the seventh game of the NBA Finals against the Golden State Warriors in 2016. It was Cleveland's first sports title in fifty-two years.

Unanimously voted Finals MVP by his teammates, James scored twenty-seven points and racked up eleven rebounds and eleven assists in the last game. As the crowd cheered, James wept as he shouted, "Cleveland, this is for you!" Still consumed with emotion, he

LeBron James's skills helped propel Cleveland to an NBA title in 2016. He succeeded in bringing a championship to his hometown team.

later told reporters, "This is what I came back for. It doesn't feel real."[43] Just a few years later, James again left Cleveland for a new team, this time landing in Los Angeles to play for the struggling Lakers.

## Danica Patrick's Big Win

In the twenty-first century, women made significant strides in sports in which they had previously been underrepresented. In 2008, Danica Patrick became the first female racecar driver to win an Indy race.

Patrick had started competing in Indy-car events, such as the famed Indianapolis 500, three years earlier. At that time, she was only the fourth woman to compete in the Indy 500 during its ninety-four-year history. After leading the race for an impressive nineteen laps—a first for a female driver—she finished in fourth place at the end of the day. Her performance during the 2005 season earned the twenty-three-year-old the title of Rookie of the Year.

Despite her obvious skills, Patrick had numerous critics, many of whom were bothered by the amount of attention she received as a female driver in the male-dominated sport. She received lucrative endorsement deals and attention from the press that male drivers with better records did not get. Allison Harthcock is a Butler University professor who teaches classes on gender and women's studies and sports media. Speaking about Patrick, Harthcock explained to *USA Today*, "Because she's not the typical driver, she gets more attention than she would if she were a male driver of comparable skill. I think that's frustrating for people."[44]

On April 26, 2008, Patrick competed in her fiftieth Indy car race, the Indy Japan 300, which was held in Motegi, Japan. At the end of the 200-lap race, Patrick was leading the pack and finished in first place. There were no more questions about whether she could or would win a race. Although it happened on foreign soil, Danica Patrick was the first woman to win a US-sanctioned open-wheel race.

Patrick was glad she would no longer have to deal with questions from the press about when it would happen. She had plenty of confidence, but she could not predict when her day would come. One person who was not surprised by her victory was Janet Guthrie, the first woman to qualify for the Indy 500, who achieved that distinction back in 1977. She told the *New York Times*, "Anybody who didn't think she had a chance of winning just hasn't been paying attention. She's been in the hunt for a long time. It was just a matter of time, as far as I'm concerned."[45]

## Phelps Just Keeps Swimming— and Winning

The Olympic Games always bring an added layer of excitement to the world of sports, but the year 2008 proved to be especially thrilling for fans of competitive swimming. For thirty-six years American swimmer Mark Spitz held the record for the most gold medals won during a single Olympics, in any sport. His seven gold medals were an impressive feat, leaving many people convinced that no one would ever beat his record. Michael Phelps, however, had a different perspective. He thought that if he worked hard enough, he could accomplish anything he set his mind to.

> "Anybody who didn't think she had a chance of winning just hasn't been paying attention. She's been in the hunt for a long time. It was just a matter of time, as far as I'm concerned."[45]
>
> — Janet Guthrie on Danica Patrick's historic Indy racing win, 2008

Phelps tied Spitz's record during the 2008 Beijing Games with his win in the men's 100-meter butterfly. He had come close to this accomplishment in the previous Summer Olympics in 2004 in Athens, but a teammate's disqualification left his tally one gold medal short at that time. In 2008, Spitz spoke to the *Today* show about the twenty-three-year-old swimmer who was poised to match his skill in the pool. "I really take my hat off to his concentration over the last four years. I mean, he really had a crack at breaking my record of seven gold medals [in 2004]. We talked about that four years ago, and unfortunately, one of the relays didn't come through for him, they didn't get the gold medal. So to stay focused for four years and to master all of the pressure that he's gotten is just remarkable."[46]

Phelps did his part, once again earning seven gold medals in the Beijing Games. But the Olympics was not yet over. He still had a chance to beat Spitz's record. Next, he swam his leg of the men's 4x100m relay for Team USA, recapturing the lead from Japan. And just as had happened in Athens, his fate now depended on the performance of one of his teammates. The entire relay team looked to Jason Lezak to finish the race first; Phelps's eighth gold was depending on it. Not only did Lezak come through for all of them, but he also helped them set a new world record for the event—3:29.34.

One person who was not at all shocked when Phelps won his historic eighth gold medal in Beijing was his coach, Bob Bowman. In an interview with CNN, Bowman shared that Phelps had trained every day for five straight years, even on birthdays and holidays. When asked how he kept up that task, Phelps said, "To be honest, it's not wanting to lose, wanting to do something no one's ever done before. That's what got me out of bed every day."[47]

# Serena's Twenty-Third Grand Slam

Serena Williams has been playing tennis since her father taught her and her older sister, Venus, the game when they were growing up. After turning pro in 1995, Serena began competing with other great athletes in the sport, including Venus. For many years the sisters ranked among the top female players on the courts worldwide, racking up valuable experience and numerous fans. Many of those fans assumed that Venus would be the first to win one of the four

Phelps has shown off his incredible power and stamina at several Olympic Games. In Beijing in 2008, he made history.

Grand Slam tournaments. These include the Australian Open, the French Open, Wimbledon, and the US Open. But Serena was the first of the two sisters to win one of these major tournaments when she won the US Open in 1999.

In the years that followed, the Williams sisters continued to make names for themselves in the sport, but Serena gradually emerged as one of the sport's greatest players. In 2002, she beat her sister in three of the four Grand Slam tournaments—the French Open, Wimbledon, and the US Open. The following year, she nabbed the

In the early twenty-first century, Serena Williams became one of the most dominant athletes of all time. She set records in tennis that will be hard to match.

only Grand Slam title she hadn't previously earned when she won the Australian Open. These wins were amazing accomplishments in themselves; taken together, they offered a hint of what was to come for the tennis superstar.

In 2014, Serena tied two other female tennis players when she won her eighteenth Grand Slam tournament. After beating Caroline Wozniacki in the US Open that year, Williams admitted, "I never dreamed that I'd be compared to Chris Evert and Martina Navratilova. I was just a kid with a dream and a racket living in Compton."[48] But the dream wasn't nearly over. She went on to rack up even more Grand Slam tournament titles, reaching a total of 23 in 2017. This was the highest number any tennis player, male or female, had ever won. Fans around the world praised Serena Williams as the greatest player in the history of the game.

In a ceremony following the 2017 Australian Open, in which she defeated Venus, Serena thanked her sister for always driving her to be her best. "Every time she won her match, I felt obligated to win—I've got to win, too. The motivation she gives me, it's really second to nothing."[49] Venus didn't miss the opportunity to support her sibling. "Serena Williams," she told everyone. "That's my little sister, guys. Your win has always been my win."[50]

Tennis enthusiasts celebrated this moment along with Serena and Venus, as they had so many of Serena's other victories on the tennis court. Fans often delight in their favorite athletes' milestones because it makes them feel a special connection to greatness. Sometimes the delight is inspired by hometown pride. Other times fans may glimpse a bit of themselves in the athletes. Top performers such as Michael Phelps or Danica Patrick have undoubtedly motivated numerous young swimmers or aspiring racecar drivers to reach for their own dreams. But even people who know they will never compete in an Olympic pool or on a racetrack relish the wins of their beloved idols. It's simply part of being a fan.

## *Fortnite* and E-Sports

One of the biggest sports stories of the early twenty-first century has been the rise of competitive video gaming—also known as E-Sports. Video games have been a popular hobby for decades. In the early days, players met up at arcades to test their skills against friends and strangers. Later, home video game consoles brought competitive gaming to couches across the world. But in the twenty-first century, the rising popularity of games and the availability of high-speed internet connections have caused the E-Sports scene to explode.

Game series like *Madden NFL*, *Call of Duty*, and *Counter-Strike* have long been known for their online play. In recent years, games like *Dota 2* and *League of Legends* have experienced global popularity and enormous prize pools rising into the tens of millions of dollars. Many top players compete in E-Sports as their full-time job.

E-Sports is about more than just the players, though. Watching streaming games online, including competitive E-Sports, has become a pastime for millions of people around the world. An estimated 380 million people watched E-Sports in 2018. The majority of them came from the United States, China, and South Korea, though fans lived all over the globe.

One of the biggest breakthroughs in competitive gaming came with the release of *Fortnite: Battle Royale* in 2017. The game soon became the most successful example of a relatively new game genre—battle royale. In battle royale games, a large number of players face off against one another on a huge map. They pick up whatever items and weapons they can find, and they are constantly forced into a smaller and smaller space on the map. The last player standing wins. *Fortnite* added a new dimension to the genre, giving players the ability to construct buildings and structures to give themselves an advantage over the competition.

*Fortnite* became one of the most successful games in history, with more than 200 million gamers registering for it. It released not only on personal computers, but also on game consoles and even smartphones. Many top players streamed themselves playing online, winning huge audiences who enjoyed not only the streamers' gameplay but their personalities. Among the biggest streamers was Ninja, whose real name is Tyler Blevins. In March 2018, he was involved in a moment that became a defining event in the history of *Fortnite*, competitive gaming, and pop culture. He was joined on a

*Fortnite* became a massive success following its 2017 launch. From huge organized competitions to individuals playing in their homes, it took over the world of competitive gaming.

*Fortnite* stream by famed Canadian rapper Drake, and the viewer count soon shot through the roof. More than 600,000 people logged in to watch. Many people felt the appearance helped bring *Fortnite* and competitive gaming to the mainstream—including Ninja. He said, "Drake, that is what pushed gaming into the mainstream and made it cool."[51]

When all is said and done, pop culture comes down to what touches people the most. Whether it is music, movies, books, sports, or gaming, everyone has something that they deeply enjoy feeling a part of. Singing along to one's favorite song will always be a part of popular culture, as will catching the latest movie or reading the latest book that everyone is raving about. As new technologies create new ways to enjoy pop culture, these things will likely become even more ingrained in our lives.

# SOURCE NOTES

## Introduction: Celebrating Pop Culture

1. Jeremy Pepper, "Comic-Con, Not Just About Comics," *USC News*, July 19, 2018. news.usc.edu.

2. Pepper, "Comic-Con, Not Just About Comics."

3. Quoted in Andrew R. Chow and Lauryn Stallings, "Their Words to Live By: Artists We Lost in 2016," *New York Times*, December 23, 2016. www.nytimes.com.

4. Quoted in Nate Jones, "Michelle Obama Explains Why Representation in Pop Culture Matters," *Variety*, August 23, 2016. www.vulture.com.

## Chapter 1: Events That Changed the World of Music

5. Quoted in "Kelly Clarkson: I Wanted to Be a Backup Singer," *CBS News*, November 18, 2015. www.cbsnews.com.

6. Michael Luca and Craig McFadden, "How Streaming Is Changing Music (Again)," *Harvard Business Review*, December 12, 2016. www.hbr.org.

7. Quoted in Jackie Willis, "Beyoncé Says She Was 'Underestimated' in Destiny's Child, Defends 'Formation' Message," *ET Online*, April 5, 2016. www.etonline.com.

8. Caroline Framke, "Beyoncé Didn't Just Steal the Super Bowl Halftime Show. She Made It a Political Act," *Vox*, February 7, 2016. www.vox.com.

9. Quoted in Dan Schawbel, "Inside the Brand of Justin Bieber: An Interview with Manager Scooter Braun," *Forbes*, February 11, 2011. www.forbes.com.

10. Desiree Abid, "Pop Star Justin Bieber Is on the Brink of Superstardom," *ABC News*, November 14, 2009. abcnews.go.com.

11. Quoted in Michael Inbar, "'Bieber Fever' Strikes Rockefeller Plaza," *Today*, June 4, 2010. www.today.com.

12. "Kanye West Ruins Taylor Swift's VMA Moment 2009," *YouTube*, September 15, 2009. www.youtube.com.

13. Quoted in Cady Lang, "A Comprehensive Guide to the Kanye West-Taylor Swift-Kim Kardashian West Feud," *Time*, July 29, 2016. www.time.com.

14. Quoted in Jenn Selby, "Kanye West in Quotes," *Independent*, December 10, 2013. www.independent.co.uk.

15. Quoted in Jillian Mapes, "Lady Gaga Explains Her Meat Dress: 'It's No Disrespect.'" *Billboard*, September 13, 2010. www.billboard.com.

16. Scott Mendelson, "Box Office: 'Suspiria' Plunges 66% As 'A Star Is Born' Passes 'The Greatest Showman.'" *Forbes*, November 11, 2018. www.forbes.com.

## Chapter 2: Television and Movies in the Twenty-First Century

17. Quoted in Anthony Jenkins, "*Survivor*'s Jeff Probst and 4 Tips for Success," *Globe and Mail*, June 9, 2013. www.theglobeandmail.com.

18. Quoted in "Showstoppers: How the Great British Bake Off Is Boosting British Business," *Chartered Management Institute*, October 7, 2015. www. managers.org.uk.

19. Quoted in Lesley Goldberg, "Why 'Grey's Anatomy' Just Overtly Tackled Unconscious Bias," *Hollywood Reporter*, January 25, 2018. www.hollywoodreporter.com.

20. Quoted in Jeanne McDowell, "A Disney Star Is Born," *Time*, November 30, 2006. content.time.com.

21. Quoted in Katie Storey, "'I Wanted to Be Clear Headed': Miley Cyrus Reveals She Has Quit Alcohol and Marijuana to Focus on New Music," *Daily Mail*, September 29, 2017. www.dailymail.co.uk.

22. Patricia Garcia, "Who Runs the World on TV? (Girls)," *Vogue*, November 18, 2014. www.vogue.com.

23. Quoted in Tara Bennett, "Geeks Embrace This 'Big Bang Theory' Too," *Today*, October 14, 2016. www.today.com.

24. Quoted in Haley Weiss, "*The Walking Dead*'s Lauren Cohan Is Set on Survival," *Interview*, October 17, 2017. www.interviewmagazine.com.

25. Quoted in Laura Bradley, "*Will & Grace* Goes Boldly into a Brave New World—But It's Hardly Changed a Thing," *Vanity Fair*, September 27, 2017. www.vanityfair.com.

26. Peter Travers, "*Star Wars: Episode II: Attack of the Clones*," *Rolling Stone*, May 16, 2002. www.rollingstone.com.

27. Quoted in Sarah Rahal, "Detroit Rapper to Host 'Black Panther' Screening for Students," *Detroit News*, February 24, 2018. www.detroitnews.com.

28. Quoted in Lindsey Bahr, "*Incredibles 2* Soars with $180 M: Biggest Opening Ever for an Animated Film," *USA Today*, June 17, 2018. www.usatoday.com.

## Chapter 3: Popular Books of the Twenty-First Century

29. Quoted in Jocelyn McClurg, "Who Will Win 'The Great American Read'? Meredith Viera, James Patterson Make Predictions," *USA Today*, September 11, 2018. www.usatoday.com.

30. Quoted in Daniel D'Addario, "George R.R. Martin on the One *Game of Thrones* Change He 'Argued Against,'" *Time*, July 13, 2017. www.time.com.

31. Quoted in Catherine Clifford, "Before 'The Martian' Became a Best Seller, Its Author Thought He'd Failed as a Writer." *CNBC*, December 11, 2017. www.cnbc.com.

32. Quoted in Charlie Lankston, "The Wild Effect: Hundreds of Women Follow in Cheryl Strayed's Footsteps and Take on 2,600-mile Pacific Crest Trail Made Famous in Her Best-Selling Novel," *Daily Mail*, December 16, 2014. www.dailymail.co.uk.

33. Quoted in Rachael Bruford, "Cheryl Strayed: From Wild to Brave Enough," *Chasing Zest*, February 1, 2018. www.chasingzest.com.

34. Quoted in Oprah Winfrey, "Michelle Obama Gets Candid with Oprah About Her New Memoir, *Becoming*." *O Magazine*, November 12, 2018. www.oprahmag.com.

35. Quoted in Brian Stelter, "Michelle Obama's 'Becoming' Sold More Than 1.4 Million Copies in First Week," *CNN*, November 21, 2018. www.cnn.com.

36. Quoted in "The *Walking Dead* Comic Book Creator Robert Kirkman Answers Fan Questions," *AMC*, 2010. www.amc.com.

37. Travis M. Andrews, "The Resurgence of Comic Books: The Industry Has Its Best-Selling Month in Nearly Two Decades," *Washington Post*, July 12, 2016. www.washingtonpost.com.

38. Quoted in Joshua Ostroff, "Superhero Diversity Takes Flight as Comic Books Fight for Gender, Race and LGBT Balance," *Huffington Post*, May 26, 2016. www.huffingtonpost.ca.

39. Quoted in Simon Armstrong, "Why Academics Are Taking Comic Books Seriously," *BBC News*, October 18, 2013. www.bbc.com.

40. Quoted in Michael Cavna, "Rare Superman Book Draws Record $3.2 Million Top Bid," *Washington Post*, August 22, 2014. www.washingtonpost.com.

# Chapter 4: Sporting Events That Have Defined the Twenty-First Century

41. Quoted in Jordan Bastian and Carrie Muskat, "Cubs Are Heavy Wait Champions!" *MLB*, November 3, 2016. www.mlb.com.

42. Quoted in Peter King, "Tom Brady on the Making of the Comeback, His Future, and Why He Doesn't Have a Grudge Against Roger Goodell," *Sports Illustrated*, September 6, 2017. www.si.com.

43. Quoted in Joshua Berlinger and Jill Martin, "Cavaliers Win NBA Championship as LeBron James Has Game of His Life," *CNN*, June 20, 2016. www.cnn.com.

44. Quoted in Matthew Van Tryon, "Why Some Fans Still Love to Hate Danica Patrick," *Indy Star*, September 18, 2017. www.indystar.com.

45. Quoted in David Caldwell, "Racing to Victory, and Leaving the Men and the Doubters Behind," *New York Times*, April 21, 2008. www.nytimes.com.

46. "Mark Spitz: 'It's Time Somebody Else Takes the Throne,'" *Today Show*, August 14, 2008. www.today.com.

47. "Michael Phelps on Making Olympic History," *CBS News*, November 25, 2008. www.cbsnews.com.

48. Quoted in Allen St. John, "Why Serena Williams Is Now the Greatest American Tennis Player Ever," *Forbes*, September 7, 2014. www.forbes.com.

49. Quoted in "Serena Williams Breaks Record with 23rd Grand Slam," *PBS News Hour*, January 28, 2017. www.pbs.org.

50. Quoted in "Serena Williams Breaks Record with 23rd Grand Slam."

51. Quoted in Brian Crecente, "Ninja: Drake Made Gaming Cool," *Variety*, December 10, 2018. www.variety.com.

# FOR FURTHER RESEARCH

## Books

Heather L. Bode. *E-Sports and the World of Competitive Gaming*. San Diego, CA: ReferencePoint Press, 2019.

Alicia Z. Klepeis. *Kanye West: Music Industry Influencer*. Minneapolis, MN: Abdo Publishing, 2018.

Jill Lepore. *The Secret History of Wonder Woman*. New York: Vintage Books, 2015.

Michael Phelps. *Beneath the Surface: My Story*. New York: Sports Publishing, 2016.

Adam Woog. *Brand Empire Celebrities*. San Diego, CA: ReferencePoint Press, 2017.

## Internet Sources

Chris Chafin, "San Diego Comic-Con: The Untold History," *Rolling Stone*, July 19, 2017. www.rollingstone.com.

Tim Gray. "Academy Nominates All White Actors for Second Year in a Row." *Variety*, January 14, 2016. www.variety.com.

Michael Rothman. "What's Driving the Resurgence of Reboots, Remakes, and Revivals in TV and Film?" *ABC News*, May 31, 2017. http://abcnews.go.com.

# Websites

### Academy Awards
**oscar.go.com**

The awards given out by the Academy of Motion Picture Arts and Sciences, known as Oscars, recognize excellence in both the technical and artistic sides of filmmaking.

### Baseball Hall of Fame
**www.baseballhall.org**

The National Baseball Hall of Fame, located in Cooperstown, New York, explores the greatest moments in the history of baseball, including those from the twenty-first century.

### Museum of Pop Culture
**www.mopop.org**

The Museum of Pop Culture, located in Seattle, Washington, features exhibits where guests can explore important people and events from music, movies, television, video games, and more.

# INDEX

*Action Comics* #1, 54
Adams, Darren, 55
Adams, Neal, 54
Amazon, 36, 48, 49, 53
*American Idol*, 10–13, 26
Andrews, Travis M., 53
Apple Computer, 15–17
auto racing, 61–63
*Avengers: Infinity War*, 53

basketball, 60–61
*Becoming*, 51
Beyoncé, 12, 17–19, 23
Bieber, Justin, 19–21
*Big Bang Theory, The*, 32–33
*Black Panther*, 8, 38–39, 54
Bowman, Bob, 64
Brady, Tom, 58–60
Braun, Scooter, 20

cable television, 36
Cara, Alessia, 21
Cartelli, Brynn, 13
Chicago Cubs, 56–58
Clarkson, Kelly, 11–13
Cleveland Cavaliers, 60
comic books, 6–7, 33, 52–55
cord cutting, 36
Cyrus, Miley, 30–31

Daft Punk, 25
*Dark Knight, The*, 53
DeGeneres, Ellen, 21, 24
Drake, 69
DVDs, 36

Epstein, Theo, 57
e-readers, 48, 49
E-Sports, 8, 67–69

*Flatliners*, 37
football, 34, 58–60
*Fortnite*, 67–69
*Fuller House*, 36

*Game of Thrones*, 45–47
Gibson, Mel, 54
*Gilmore Girls*, 35
*Great American Read, The*, 42–43
*Great British Baking Show, The*, 28
*Grey's Anatomy*, 28–29
Guthrie, Janet, 62

*Hannah Montana*, 29–31
*Harry Potter*, 42–44
Hudson, Jennifer, 13
Hulu, 36

*Incredibles, The*, 39–40
*Incredibles 2*, 40–41
iPod, 15–16

Jackson, Michael, 21–22
James, LeBron, 60–61
Jay-Z, 18
Jenkins, Henry, 8

Kaepernick, Colin, 59
Kardashian, Kim, 24
Kindle, 49
Kirkman, Robert, 53

Lady Gaga, 24–25
Lamar, Kendrick, 39
Lambert, Adam, 13
Los Angeles Lakers, 61
Louis-Dreyfus, Julia, 32

*Martian, The*, 47–48
Martin, George R.R., 45–47
Mendes, Shawn, 21
Messing, Debra, 35
Miami Heat, 60
*Murphy Brown*, 35
music formats, 13–14

Napster, 14–15
Netflix, 36
New England Patriots, 58–60
Ninja, 68–69

Obama, Michelle, 9, 51–52
*Ocean's Eleven*, 37
Olympic Games, 63–64, 67
*One Day at a Time*, 36
*Outlander*, 43

Pandora, 17
Patrick, Danica, 61–63
Patterson, James, 42–43
Phelps, Michael, 63–64, 67
Pixar, 39–41
Prince, 9
Probst, Jeff, 27
Puth, Charlie, 21

*Queer Eye*, 36

remakes, 25, 35–37
Rowling, J.K., 42–43

San Diego Comic-Con, 6–8
Seacrest, Ryan, 12
Sia, 25
*Song of Ice and Fire, A*, 45–47
Spears, Britney, 10
Spitz, Mark, 63–64
Spotify, 17
*Star Is Born, A*, 25
*Star Wars*, 37
Strayed, Cheryl, 49–51
Super Bowl, 18, 58–59
superhero movies, 6–7, 33, 37–41,
    52–53
*Survivor*, 26–28
Swift, Taylor, 22–23
swimming, 63–64

Tee Grizzley, 39
tennis, 64–67
*To Kill a Mockingbird*, 43
*True Grit*, 37

# INDEX CONTINUED

Underwood, Carrie, 12

video games, 7, 43, 67–69
Video Music Awards, 22, 24
vinyl records, 13, 17

*Walking Dead, The*, 33–35, 53, 54
Weir, Andy, 47–48
West, Kanye, 22–24
*West Wing, The*, 31
*Wild*, 50–51
*Will & Grace*, 35
Williams, Serena, 64–67
Williams, Venus, 64, 67
Winfrey, Oprah, 51
Witherspoon, Reese, 51
Wonder Woman, 8, 53
World Series, 56–58
Wright, Robin, 32

young adult novels, 43–44
YouTube, 8, 20–21

Zendaya, 39
zombies, 33–35

# IMAGE CREDITS

# ABOUT THE AUTHOR

Tammy Gagne has written dozens of books for both adults and children. Her recent titles include *Online Shaming and Bullying* and *Women in the Workplace*. She lives in northern New England with her husband, her son, and a menagerie of pets.